Mastering Your

Introduction to

Cyber Security

Dr. Michael C. Redmond, PhD
Retired Lieutenant Colonel, US Army
MBCP, FBCI, CEM, PMP

Certified as Lead Implementer:
- ISO/IEC 27001 Information Security Management
- ISO/IEC 27032 Lead Cyber Security Manager
- ISO/IEC 27035 Security Incident Response
- ISO/IEC 22301 Business Continuity Management
- ISO/IEC 21500 Lead Project Manager
- ISO 31000 Risk Management

Certified as Lead Auditor:
- ISO/IEC 27001 Information Security Management
- ISO/IEC 22301 Business Continuity Management

Hardcover ISBN: 978-1-63491-543-4
Paperback ISBN: 978-1-63491-418-5

Published by BookLocker.com, Inc., Bradenton, Florida.

Printed on acid-free paper.

BookLocker.com, Inc.
2018

First Edition

BookLocker

Dedication

To my daughter Brie, whom I love unconditionally!

Acknowledgement

Thanks Angie Mangino, for being a great editor.

Thanks Tom Martin, for your help with proofreading.

DISCLAIMER

This book details the author's personal experiences with and opinions about an introduction to cyber security.

The author and publisher are providing this book and its contents on an "as is" basis and make no representations or warranties of any kind with respect to this book or its contents. The author and publisher disclaim all such representations and warranties, including for example warranties of merchantability and information security and cyber advice for a particular purpose. In addition, the author and publisher do not represent or warrant that the information accessible via this book is accurate, complete or current.

The statements made about products and services have not been evaluated by the U.S. government. Please consult with your own legal or accounting professional regarding the suggestions and recommendations made in this book.

Except as specifically stated in this book, neither the author or publisher, nor any authors, contributors, or other representatives will be liable for damages arising out of or in connection with the use of this book. This is a comprehensive limitation of liability that applies to all damages of any kind, including (without limitation) compensatory; direct, indirect or consequential damages; loss of data, income or profit; loss of or damage to property and claims of third parties.

You understand that this book is not intended as a substitute for consultation with a licensed medical, legal or accounting professional. Before you begin any change of your lifestyle in any way, consult a licensed professional to ensure that you are doing what's best for your situation.

This book provides content related to Cyber Security and information security topics. As such, use of this book implies your acceptance of this disclaimer.

Table of Contents

Table of Contents

Dr. Michael C. Redmond, PhD

About the Author

Dr. Michael C. Redmond, PhD is CEO of Redmond Worldwide, an International Consulting Company and consults, trains and audits in the areas of Cyber Program Management including Cyber Security Incident Response, Cyber Programs development, and training, SIEM – Security Information and Event Management. In addition, the company also consults in Business Continuity, Disaster Recovery, and Crisis Management.

The company can be accessed for more Information at www.redmondworldwide.com. Prior consulting experience includes both consulting and compliance auditing with such firms as Chubb, Deloitte and KPMG. She served four years on Active Duty with the U.S. Military and completed an additional 16 years with the National Guard and Reserve.

She is a Consultant, Trainer, Speaker, and Author. Michael also conducts ISO Certification Training for PECB. Michael an active member of Information Systems Security Association

(ISSA), ISACA, Project management Institute (PMI), Association of Contingency Planners and Contingency Planning Exchange. She has consulted and audited in the area of Cyber Security for clients internationally in the arenas of Healthcare, Insurance, Finance, and Manufacturing. Her projects have included:

- ❖ Compliance, Risk and Governance
- ❖ Developing full Cyber and Information Security Programs and Implementation
- ❖ SIEM Security Information and Event Management
- ❖ (CSIRT) Cyber Security Incident Response Programs, Plans, Playbooks, Training and Testing
- ❖ Table Top Tests
- ❖ Testing and Exercises
- ❖ Audit of Programs and Documentation
- ❖ Preparing Organizations for Certification
- ❖ Certification Audits
- ❖ Audit of CSIRT Programs and Documentation
- ❖ SIEM Security Information and Event Management - Combining software products and services combining security information management (SIM) and security event management (SEM)
- ❖ ISO Certification Trainer
- ❖ ISO Implementer Certification Training
- ❖ ISO Audit Certification Training
- ❖ Audit of CSIRT programs and documentation

She has been honored as a Top Woman in her field at a White House Luncheon and was selected out of the world to write the prologue for the chapter on RISK Management by the United Nations for their Disaster Book, which was given to the head of state for every UN member nation. Women of Distinction

Magazine named her on the list of "Women of Distinction for 2017" for her work in Cyber Security.

She served for a short time as the US Attaché to Chile for Disaster Recovery at the request of the President of Chile.

She is a Certified Business Recovery Planner; Certified Emergency Manager; and holds two Master Level Certifications in Business Continuity. She has ISO Certifications as Lead Implementer and Auditor.

Certified as Lead Implementer:

ISO/IEC 27001 Information Security Management
ISO/IEC 27032 Lead Cyber Security Manager
ISO/IEC 27035 Security Incident Response
ISO/IEC 22301 Business Continuity Management Systems
ISO/IEC 21500 Lead Project Manager
ISO 31000 Risk Management
ISO 55001 Asset Management
ISO/IEC 14001 Environmental Management
ISO 9001 Quality Management
ISO 26000 Social Responsibility
ISO 37001 Anti Bribery Management Systems

Certified Implementer – Foundation

ISO 22316 Resiliency Management
ISO 22320 Emergency Management
ISO 20700 Management Consultancy Services

Certified as Lead Auditor:

ISO/IEC 27001 Information Security Management
ISO/IEC 22301 Business Continuity Management Systems
ISO 55001 Asset Management
ISO/IEC 14001 Environmental Management
ISO 9001 Quality Management
ISO 26000 Social Responsibility

Other Certifications:

Masters Business Continuity Planning (Disaster Recovery Institute) - MBCP
Masters Business Continuity Planning (Business Continuity Institute) - FBCI
Certified Emergency Manager - CEM
Certified Project Manager – PMP
Certified Trainer PECB

She is also a graduate of Command & General Staff College out of Fort Leavenworth, where she studied strategic planning, control and command, and control in an emergency. Furthermore, she has completed Civil Affairs Advanced courses in the School for Special Warfare, which encompasses planning in various political and cultural environments.

She was an Adjunct Professor for Emergency Management and Business Continuity Management at New York University and the Masters program at John Jay College.

Dr. Redmond is an author and an International Speaker. She has written for many Contingency, Risk and Security magazines and has Audio Training Programs on Cyber Security and Business Continuity/Disaster Recovery and Emergency Management COOP and COG. Michael's Audio Trainings receive Continuing Education Units/Points (CEU) and (CEP) from Disaster Recovery Institute (DRI) and other certifying organizations.

❖ Cyber Security Training - 6 CEU's/CEP's
❖ Business Continuity Management - 20 CEU's/CEP's

www.rwknowledge.com

Prologue

In addition to consulting, I conduct many Webinars, write articles, and speak on the subject of Cyber Security. This topic is a must today!

The world we live in is highly dominated by modern technology. The most important technologies, and probably the most advanced, are found in the cyber world. Thus, knowledge about the cyber world has begun to gain even more importance.

There is so much to know about the cyber world. It is a huge network of terminology and definitions. The introduction of the internet has made our lives easier. Not surprisingly, Cyber Security is becoming one of the most important departments in many organizations.

Fortunately, a minimum knowledge in this field could reduce the chances of cybercrime and provide a safer environment. This book is a must for those wanting an introduction to gain general knowledge about Cyber Security.

Introduction

There are so many Cyber attacks around the world, and so few people understand how or why. Companies, countries, militaries, and individuals are all fair game in a Cyber Attack. There is a vast need for knowledge in this area. Many organizations now realize knowledge of the basic concepts is critical if they are going to be able to mitigate the risk and damage from attacks.

This book serves as an introduction to Cyber Security for employees, managers, students and for IT, Information Security, Business Continuity and Disaster Recovery professionals. Individuals in all organizations, including Private and Public Sectors, will benefit from understanding the clearly explained introduction to Cyber Security.

The Self-Training that you are undertaking using this book is an introduction to Information and Cyber Security. This is truly an introduction, but the information is still plentiful, since there is so much to know and to understand. After reading this book, you will understand Cyber Threats such as viruses, worms, malware, breach, denial of service and so much more.

There is a self-test at the end of the book for each of the chapters and the answers are provided in a separate answer section.

Introduction to Cyber Security Planning is based on best practice regulations and compliance, including, but not limited to: COBIT, Federal Financial Institutions Examination Council (FFIEC), Cybersecurity Guidebook for Cyber-Physical Vehicle

Systems SAE J3061_201601, Estonia Ministry of Economic Affairs and Communication Strategy, Federal Information Security Management Act (FISMA), European Union Agency for Network and Information Security (ENISA), Gramm-Leach-Bliley Act (GLBA), Health Insurance Portability and Accountability Act (HIPAA), International Organization for Standardization (ISO), National Cyber Security Strategy (NCSS), North American Electric Reliability Corporation Critical Infrastructure Plan (NERC CIP), National Institute of Standards and Technology (NIST), Payment Card Industry Data Security Standard (PCI DSS), and Sarbanes-Oxley Act (SOX).To assist you in developing or assessing an existing program, the standards will be combined with other guidelines and industry specific best practices.

Please note that while the SANS Institute, which was established in 1989, is not a source of standards per se, it is a cooperative research and education organization that many entities use for guidance on best practices.

Chapter 1: Cyber Security Standards

About this Chapter

Many industries and government agencies utilize different standards, regulations and best practices. I have compiled this list to help you in understanding standards, regulations and best practices that are part of the Cyber Security arena.

Control Objectives for Information and Related Technology (COBIT)

COBIT As per ISACA.org, is an IT governance framework and supporting toolset that allows managers to bridge the gap between control requirements, technical issues and business risks. COBIT enables clear policy development and good practice for IT controls throughout organizations. COBIT emphasizes regulatory compliance, helps organizations to increase the value attained from IT, enables alignment and simplifies implementation of enterprises' IT governance and control framework. COBIT 5 consolidates and integrates the COBIT 4.1, Val IT 2.0 and Risk IT frameworks and also draws significantly from the Business Model for Information Security (BMIS) and ITAF.

Cybersecurity Guidebook for Cyber-Physical Vehicle Systems (SAE J3061_201601)

Cyber Security recommended practice for the vehicle industry, as well as to other cyber-physical vehicle systems (e.g., commercial and military vehicles, trucks, busses).

Estonia Ministry of Economic Affairs and Communication Strategy

Provides NATO nations and partners with Cyber Security guidelines in implementing their programs.

European Union Agency for Network and Information Security (ENISA)

Maintains a list of National Cyber Security Strategy Documents in the EU and, in addition, includes many other non-EU countries.

Federal Financial Institutions Examination Council (FFIEC)

As per ffiec.com, the Council is a formal interagency body empowered to prescribe uniform principles, standards, and report forms for the federal examination of financial institutions by the Board of Governors of the Federal Reserve System (FRB), the Federal Deposit Insurance Corporation (FDIC), the National Credit Union Administration (NCUA), the Office of the Comptroller of the Currency (OCC), and the Consumer Financial Protection Bureau (CFPB), and to make recommendations to promote uniformity in the supervision of financial institutions.

Federal Information Security Management Act (FISMA)

Promotes the development of key security standards and guidelines to support the implementation of and compliance with the Federal Information Security Management Act including:

❖ Guidance for assessing security controls in information systems and determining security control effectiveness
❖ Guidance for monitoring the security controls and the security authorization of information systems
❖ Guidance for selecting appropriate security controls for information systems
❖ Guidance for the security authorization of information systems

Gramm-Leach-Bliley Act (GLBA)

As per ftc.gov, the Gramm-Leach-Bliley Act requires financial institutions – companies that offer consumers financial products or services like loans, financial or investment advice, or insurance – to explain their information-sharing practices to their customers and to safeguard sensitive data.

Health Insurance Portability and Accountability Act (HIPAA)

Security rule within the U.S that outlines how security should be managed for any facility that creates, accesses, shares, or destroys medical information. Ensures appropriate protection of electronic protected health information.

National Cyber Security Strategy (NCSS)

Cyber Security approach for European Union that prioritizes and provides timelines for national Cyber Security objectives. Many countries in Europe have their own Cyber Security Strategy.

National Institute of Standards and Technology (NIST)

NIST advances measurement science, standards, and technology in ways that enhance economic security and improve quality of life. Its mission is to promote U.S. innovation and industrial competitiveness. NIST is a non-regulatory federal agency within the U.S. Department of Commerce.

North American Electric Reliability Corporation Critical Infrastructure Plan (NERC CIP)

As per nerc.com, NERC CIP consists of 9 standards and 45 requirements covering the security of electronic perimeters and the protection of critical cyber assets, as well as personnel and training, security management and disaster recovery planning. The mission of the North American Electric Reliability Corporation (NERC) is ensuring the security and reliability of the electric grid. With the approval of Federal Energy Regulatory Commission, this addresses the security of cyber assets essential to the reliable operation of the electric grid.

Payment Card Industry Data Security Standard (PCI DSS)

As per PCI Security Standards, PCI DSS, a set of comprehensive requirements for enhancing payment account data security was developed by the founding payment brands of the PCI Security Standards Council, including American Express, Discover Financial Services, MasterCard Worldwide and Visa Inc. International, to help facilitate the broad adoption of consistent data security measures on a global basis.

Sarbanes-Oxley Act (SOX)

As per sec.gov, SOX provides information, and identifies resources, to help ensure successful audit, and management. Compliance with the legislation requires it to be addressed methodically. Some sections apply more to compliance than others.

International Organization for Standardization (ISO)

International Organization for Standardization (ISO) has a family of standards that apply to Information Security, Cyber Security, as well as Risk Management. The list below is from that family and you may wish to review others also. ISO has published over 21,655 International Standards and related documents.

Some of the other ISO standards that I recommend include some different views related to information technology and security techniques. After each of the ISO numbers will be a colon that is followed by the most recent year. For purposes of this book, I have left the years off to keep the material from being dated and depicted them as: 20XX.

International Electrotechnical Commission (IEC) is a not for profit organization not related to a Government Agency. Any Standards that they develop jointly with ISO will have ISO/IEC in the title. They produce standards connected to electro technology.

The ISO/IEC 27000 series covers Information Technology, Security techniques, Information Security Management Systems and overview and vocabulary.

Some of the individual ISO standards that you will find helpful when implementing or auditing Cyber Security are listed here.

Individual Standards:

ISO/IEC 27001:20XX covers:
- ❖ Information Security Management System Requirements

ISO/IEC 27002:20XX covers:
- ❖ Code of Practice for Information Security Management
- ❖ Information Technology
- ❖ Security Techniques

ISO/IEC 27003:20XX covers:
- ❖ Information Security Management System Implementation Guidance
- ❖ Information Technology
- ❖ Security Techniques

ISO/IEC 27004:20XX: covers:
- ❖ Information Security Management
- ❖ Information Technology
- ❖ Measurement
- ❖ Security techniques

ISO/IEC 27005:20XX covers:
- ❖ Information Security Risk Management
- ❖ Information Technology
- ❖ Security Techniques

ISO/IEC 27007:20XX covers:
- ❖ Guidelines For Information Security Management Systems Auditing
- ❖ Information Technology
- ❖ Security Techniques

ISO/IEC 29100:20XX covers:
- ❖ Common Privacy Terminology
- ❖ Privacy Safeguards And Considerations
- ❖ Privacy Principles For Known Technology

ISO/IEC 38500:20XX covers:
- ❖ Information Technology Governance
- ❖ Required Performance
- ❖ Respect for the Human Factors

Chapter 2: What's In Place

About this Chapter

It's essential to learn what is already in place related to Cyber Security in an organization. Knowing who the key players and stakeholders are makes being compliant with the organization a much easier task.

Cyber Security is a necessity in today's world. Cyber attacks have increased exponentially in sophistication, as well as domination across the threat landscape. Cyber warfare is affecting countries around the world. Financial information is being stolen at a rapid pace. The world's continuous dependency upon technology, and the rapid increase in the complexities of these technologies, makes securing them a challenge and an urgent requirement. We need to understand all the threats and dangers we are vulnerable to, and the counter measures that are in place to mitigate risk. Penetration studies demonstrate the level of threats that exist throughout organizations. Without these studies, there would be a false sense of security.

Information Assurance (IA) practitioners seek to protect and defend information systems by ensuring confidentiality, integrity, authentication, availability, and non-repudiation. These goals are relevant whether the information is processing, in storage, or in transit. IA is the process of ensuring that authorized users have access to information at the authorized time.

Key Questions to Ask

Key questions to ask oneself before starting to Plan are:

- ❖ Who are the key members?
  - o Who should be included?
- ❖ What information does the organization not want employees accessing from home?
- ❖ What are some "how to" areas that have to be considered from a documentation point of view?
  - o Access Control
  - o Asset Management, Human Resources Security
  - o Business Continuity Management
  - o Classification
  - o Communications And Operations Management
  - o Containment
  - o Defining A Reportable Incident
  - o Defining A Security Incident
  - o Defining Roles, Responsibilities And Lines Of Authority
  - o Detection
  - o Development and Maintenance
  - o Documentation
  - o Eradication
  - o Escalation
  - o Information Security Incident Management
  - o Information Systems Acquisition
  - o Organization of Information Security
  - o Physical and Environmental Security
  - o Policy
  - o Regulatory Compliance
  - o Selecting Team Members

      o   Training

When There is a Plan

If there is a Cyber Security Plan, ask the following questions:

- ❖ Does information considered critical by the organization include security mitigation, protection, and recoverability of data?
- ❖ Does it identify teams needed?
- ❖ Has the plan ever been tested along with the Continuity Plan?
- ❖ How are team members selected?
- ❖ How are vendors' Cyber Security Plans evaluated?
- ❖ How many times has the organization tested the security in a secure environment, as opposed to a mock disaster where chaos is an added factor in the security testing?
- ❖ Is mandatory continued education included?

Chart to Assist in Determining What is in Place

Organizations must practice safe security techniques in order to minimize the number of successful Cyber Security attacks. Although security awareness among organizations is increasing, the rise in security threats to organizations also puts national infrastructure at risk, according to experts. This chart depicts a process for evaluating what is in place and the aspects that are important for each.

Aspect	Focus	Target audience	Issues probed	Scope and coverage
Computer Installations	A computer deployment of software that supports one or more business applications	The CI target audience include: Owners of application installations Individuals accountable for maintaining data centers IT managers Third parties that operate company assets and installations for the business. IT auditors	Develop risk preventative measures by integrating best practice requirements for key business applications & services to meet corporate compliance goals.	Computer installations: Of all size & scope (including the largest mainframe, server-based systems, and groups of workstations) Running in specialized environments (e.g., a purpose-built data center), or in ordinary working environments (e.g., offices, factories, and warehouses)
Critical Business Applications	A business application that is critical to the success of the enterprise.	The CB target audience include: - Owners of business applications - Individuals in charge of business processes that are dependent on applications - Systems integrators - Technical staff, such as members of an application support team.	The security requirements of the application and the preventive measures made for identifying risk and keeping them within acceptable levels.	Critical business applications: Coverage (including transaction processing, process control, funds transfer, customer service, and workstation applications) Scope (e.g., applications supporting thousands of users or just a few)
Security Management (enterprise-wide)	Security management at enterprise level.	The SM target audience include: - Heads of security functions (or equivalent) - Information security managers - IT auditors	The commitment to deliver good information security best practices across the enterprise by upper management, along with the allocation of appropriate resources.	Security management organization within: A group of businesses (or equivalent) Part of a group (e.g., subsidiary company or business unit) An individual organization (e.g., a company or a government department)

Aspect	Focus	Target audience	Issues probed
End User Environment	An environment (e.g., a business unit or department) in which individuals use corporate resources and assets to support business processes.	The target audience includes: ▪ Business managers ▪ Individuals in the end-user environment ▪ Local information-security coordinators ▪ Information-security managers (or equivalent)	The arrangements for user education and awareness. Proper use of corporation applications and critical protection of information across enterprise.
Systems Development	A systems development unit, department, or a particular systems development project.	The target audience include: ▪ Heads of systems development functions ▪ System developers ▪ IT auditors	How business needs are identified (including information security requirements); and how systems are designed and built to meet those needs.
Networks	A network that supports one or more business applications	The target audience includes: Heads of specialist network functions Network managers Third parties that provide network services (e.g., Internet service providers) IT auditors	How requirements for network services are identified and how the networks are set up to meet those business goals and needs.

Chapter 3: Risks and Mitigations

About this Chapter

Cyber Security has its own inherent risks that can be mitigated, if not prevented. Understanding these risks and mitigations helps an organization strategize better.

Why Have Cyber Security?

The world today relies greatly on computing systems and the Internet for communication (email, mobile phones), entertainment (digital cable, mp3s), transportation (car engine systems, airplane navigation), shopping (online stores, credit cards), medicine (equipment, medical records), and it doesn't end here as technology grows to tailor our daily lifestyle choices. How much of our daily lives rely on computers? How much of our personal information is stored either on company owned systems, embedded applications, or within someone else's system?

Cyber security involves protecting that information by detecting, preventing and responding to attacks. It is a development of processes and best practices designed to protect networks, computers, programs and data damage or unauthorized access.

What Are The Risks?

There are many risks, some more severe than others. These dangers range from viruses erasing an entire system to someone breaking into the systems. Attackers are known for altering files, using the computer to attack others, stealing identities, and using others credit card and financial information to make unauthorized purchases. Attackers can open up other fake accounts and businesses utilizing this information in order to maximize gain. Even with the best protections, some of these things can happen to any organization or person. This is why it is important to establish best practice solutions. These solutions should be a part of the secure environment in order to minimize risk.

Security Policy

Human error causes most problems. Raising security awareness within the organization can help with mitigation. Government and organizational laptops are being lost, with sensitive data often finding its way into the public domain.

People often move corporate data around, perhaps sending it home for out-of-hours work, or forwarding it to a friend because there was something funny in it.
This is done without malice, but in ways that expose an organization to potential security and legal risk.

Better education for users would help eradicate these threats. Staff must be aware of their responsibilities regarding company and customer data, and there must be enforcement and adherence to policies.

Allow employees to have only approved software on their laptops and computer. Instruct employees to lockdown computers at the end of the night. Computers should be set up to allow lockdown by control/alt/delete or other such conformity.

Employee policies should prohibit access to unauthorized websites. In addition, the policy should prohibit opening, and especially passing along, emails that contain moving graphics. Employee abuse of email, instant messaging, and surfing for porn, eBay, sports and news sites is costing organizations lost productivity every year, but more importantly, it opens the organization to cyber terrorism. When employees know close monitoring exists, they drastically reduce the activities that harm your business. Consider a monitoring tool to reduce the risk and to enforce the security policy.

Cyber Terrorism or Cyber Attack?

"Attacker", "intruder", and "hacker" are terms applied to people who seek to exploit weaknesses in software and computer systems for their own gain. Although their intentions are sometimes fairly benign and motivated solely by curiosity, their actions are typically in violation of the intended use of the systems they are exploiting. The results vary from altering data, stealing, to no impact.

The FBI defines terrorism as the unlawful use of force or violence against persons or property to intimidate or coerce a government, the civilian population, or any segment thereof, in furtherance of political or social objectives. Cyber attacks can be for political, financial, espionage and other reasons.

Both cyber-terrorism and cyber attacks can result in the use of using resources to intimidate or coerce others. An example of cyber-terrorism could be hacking into a hospital computer system to change someone's medicine prescription to a lethal dosage as an act of revenge. These things can and do happen.

Cyber attacks are becoming a viable option to traditional physical acts of violence due to:
- Anonymity
- Diverse targets
- Ease of operation from nearly any location
- Fewer resources are needed
- Low risk of detection
- Low risk of personal injury
- Low investment

Getting Started

List the main information that the organization does not want anyone to have. The areas under Cyber Security are broken down into hardware, software, network, automation, the users and the suppliers. Deal with the human side of Cyber Security in procedures. If you are doing business with a country that does not even have Cyber Security laws, then the risk is even higher. Malicious attacks are plentiful today.

Unfortunately, some individuals exploit the Internet through criminal behavior and other harmful acts. Criminals can try to gain unauthorized access to users' computers and then use that access to steal identities, commit fraud, or even launch cyber attacks against your organization. By following Cyber Security practices, users can mitigate the harm cyber criminals can cause. In adapting a security program, remember every PC is a possible area for attack.

Only the organization can determine what is actually at risk. If a thief steals a laptop, the most obvious loss is the machine itself. However, if the thief is able to access the information on the computer , all of the information stored on the device is at risk, as well as any additional accessed information of the data stored on the device itself.

Unauthorized people should not be able to access sensitive corporate information or customer account information. Even if there is not any sensitive corporate information on a laptop, think of the other information at risk: information about appointments, passwords, email addresses and other contact information, personal information for organization accounts, etc.

Awareness sessions for users are a good way to start. Cover such topics as

- ❖ Choosing and Protecting Passwords
- ❖ Understanding Anti-Virus Software
- ❖ Understanding Firewalls
- ❖ Coordination Virus and Spyware Defense
- ❖ Protect the organizations laptops
- ❖ Password-protect all computers. Make sure that users have to enter a password to log in to the computer
- ❖ Users should keep the laptop with them at all times. When traveling, users should keep their laptop with them at all times unless required by the airline to check the laptop. Meal times are optimum times for thieves to check hotel rooms for unattended laptops. If users are attending a conference or trade show, they must be especially wary. These venues offer thieves a wider selection of devices that are likely to contain sensitive information, and the conference sessions offer more opportunities for thieves to access guest rooms.
- ❖ Downplay laptops. There is no need for users to advertise to thieves that they have a laptop. When

possible, consider non-traditional bags for carrying laptops.

❖ Back up files. Someone else may be able to access information from a stolen device. To avoid losing all of the information, users should make incremental backups of important information and store the backups in a separate location until they can back up the information on the organizations system. Not only will they still be able to access the information, but also they will be able to identify and report exactly what information is at risk.

❖ Laptop Users Guidelines while on the road if unable to backup to the organization's backup system

  o Make sure users do a fire drill to make sure your backup system is working. It is astonishing how many users, when it comes time to restore, discover their backup are empty or are missing crucial data.

  o Keep offsite backups. If a user's computer in their office is damaged by fire, flood or theft, chances are, their individual onsite backups wi

Physical Security Is an Important Part of Cyber Security

Today's headlines include Data Breach, Denial of Service and so much more. Cyber Security and Risk Management is not only about preventing external attacks, but also identifying and protecting against the insider threat.

Passwords

One of the best ways to protect information or physical property is to ensure that only authorized people have access to it. Verifying that someone is the person they claim to be is the next step, and this authentication process is even more important, and more difficult, in the cyber world. Passwords are the most common means of authentication, but if users do not choose good passwords or keep them confidential, they are almost as ineffective as not having any password at all. Many systems and services have been successfully broken into due to the use of insecure and inadequate passwords, and some viruses and worms have exploited systems by guessing weak passwords.

Anti-Virus Software

Antivirus Software is an essential security application. Most antivirus products can remove detected malicious code and repair most damage caused by such malicious code. It's one example of a host IDS. It monitors the local system for evidence of malware in memory, in active processes, and in storage.

In order for antivirus software to be effective, it must be kept current with daily signature-database updates. It is also important to use the most recent engine, because new methods of detection and removal are found only in the most current versions of antivirus software.

Once an organization installs an anti-virus package, users should scan their entire computer periodically.

> ❖ Automatic scans - Depending on what software the organization chooses, they may be able to configure it to automatically scan specific files or directories and prompt at set intervals to perform complete scans.

❖ Manual scans - It is also a good idea to have users manually scan files received from an outside source before opening them. This includes

   o saving and scanning email attachments or web downloads rather than selecting the option to open them directly from the source
   o scanning media, including CDs and DVDs, for viruses before opening any of the files

Firewalls

A firewall is a hardware or software component designed to protect one network from another. Firewalls provide protection by controlling traffic entering and leaving a network. Firewalls are typically deployed between areas of high and low trust zones, like a private network communicating to the public internet or between two networks that belong to the same organization, but are from different departments.

Spyware and Viruses

Spyware and viruses can interfere with an organization's ability to process information or can modify or destroy data. Some organizations believe that the more anti-virus and anti-spyware programs they install on the network and individual remote computers, the safer they will be. It is true that not all programs are equally effective, and they will not all detect the same malicious code. However, it is possible to introduce problems by installing multiple programs in an attempt to catch everything.

Malicious Code

Malicious code is a set of instructions designed to compromise the system, mobile device, laptop, desktop, server and other electronic systems that can run code. This category includes code such as viruses, worms, and Trojan horses. Although some people use these terms interchangeably, they have unique characteristics.

- ❖ Viruses – Any malicious software that is designed to affect system storage files, memory and running processes.
- ❖ Worms – Similar to a virus except that it propagates the virus so that it can spread across the network
- ❖ Trojan horses – Malicious software that hides itself as legitimate software. It masquerades as actual software, but it actually has remote controlled software underneath.
- ❖ Rootkits – Rootkits are ring 0 (Kernel Mode) / ring 3 (User Mode) that operate at the highest privilege level of the system designed to subvert the Operating System in an attempt to remain hidden from detection from the kernel.
- ❖ Exploit Kits – Exploit kits are obfuscated codes, which serve as toolkits used to exploit security holes, primarily within the browser, to further spread infection malware.

Chapter 4: Impacts and Preparation

About this Chapter

Cyber events and incidents can have an impact on an organization. Understanding these potential impacts helps an organization prepare before an event or incident occurs.

One of the biggest obstacles in defending against Cyber Security crime is in the disparity across international regulations. There are no borders in cyberspace. This is why domestic laws cannot address this problem. The International Multilateral Partnership Against Cyber Threats (IMPACT) is the first United Nations-backed cybersecurity alliance. This was the first international treaty on crimes committed via the Internet. Since 2011, IMPACT serves as a key partner of the United Nations (UN). The United States and India signed a Memorandum of Understanding (MOU) Cyber Security Agreement in July 2011. The Council of Europe (CoE) Cybercrime went into force on July 1, 2004. The United States and China signed a Cyber Agreement September 25, 2015.

Preparations Before an Event or Incident

- ❖ Application Security
    - ○ It is essential to segregate conflicting duties and protect sensitive information through appropriate security principles for applications.

- Process & Systems Integrity Implementation
- Application Security Reviews
- Business Cycle Control Reviews
- Pre and Post-Implementation Reviews
- Healthcheck Reviews

❖ Information Security and Risk Management
  - o Establish security policy
  - o Assess risk to better understand vulnerabilities
  - o Implement the right amount of protection
  - o Measure and enforce compliance

❖ Legal, Regulations, Compliance and Investigations (From (ISC) 2 Candidate Information Bulletin)
  - o Legal, Regulations, Compliance and Investigations addresses computer crime laws and regulations; the investigative measures and techniques which can be used to determine if a crime has been committed, methods to gather evidence if it has, as well as the ethical issues of code and conduct for the security professional.
  - o Incident handling provides the ability to react quickly and efficiently to malicious threats or incidents.

❖ Operations Security
❖ Physical (Environmental) Security
❖ Security Architecture and Design
❖ Telecommunications and Network Security

Cyber Security Incident Response (CSIRT)

Process of developing and documenting Programs, Plans, Procedures that enable an organization to respond to an Incident that can threaten the organization, information and clients.

CSIRT Set Up Steps
The steps in setting up a Cyber Security Incident Response (CSIRT) include:

- ❖ Project Initiation and Management
- ❖ Cyber Impact Analysis
- ❖ Developing Cyber Strategies
- ❖ Emergency Response and Operations
- ❖ Developing and Implementing Cyber Plans
- ❖ Awareness Programs and Training
- ❖ Maintaining and Exercising the Cyber Plans
- ❖ Crisis Communications
- ❖ Coordination with External Agencies

Chapter 5: The Attack

About this Chapter

Understanding about the potential Cyber Enemies and how they may attack is critical to planning.

Critical Infrastructures are those systems or assets, whether physical or virtual, that if debilitated or incapacitated would have a debilitating effect. This is an area most threatened and easily fits within the targeted criteria of an attacker.

The Computer Crime Research Center, which was created in 2001, conducts research in criminological problems of cybercrime and legal criminal implications. The Computer Crime Research Center (CCRC) is a scientific research, non-governmental and non-profit organization. They collaborate with The Security Engineering Research Center (SERC), The Zaporizhzhya National University "ZNU" (Zaporozhye, Ukraine) Hannam University (Korea) and other universities, institutes and research centers.

The Computer Crime Research Center states, "Any person who commits an illegal act with a guilty intention or commits a crime is called an offender or a criminal." In this context, any person who commits a Cyber Crime is known as a Cyber Criminal. They further state, "Cyber Criminals may possibly be children and adolescents and teenagers, organized hackers, may be professional hackers or crackers, discontented employees, or others."

Cyber Attackers can be a dissident group or faction, individual, a criminal organization or another country. Attacks can be generated externally or internally and may be focus on the supporting infrastructure (telecommunications, electricity, etc.), or be generated directly against a computer system.

Cyber Attacks can take the form of:

- ❖ Denial or disruption of computer, cable, satellite, or telecommunications services
- ❖ Disclosure of private, classified, or proprietary information communicated or stored within computer, cable, satellite, or telecommunications systems
- ❖ Modification or destruction of computer programming codes, computer network databases, stored information, or computer capabilities
- ❖ Manipulation of computer, cable, satellite, or telecommunications services resulting in fraud, financial loss, or other criminal violation
- ❖ Threats to destroy data or program files

What Can Be Done?

Manage vulnerabilities using a variety of cost-effective countermeasures readily available.

Passwords are a simple, yet still necessary provision. Users should be required to use a combination of letters, numbers, and large and small case. Case sensitive passwords are best. In the same vein, upgrading vendor software to include higher security features is a critical practice. Have controls in place ahead of time to include policies such as the use of encryption.

Implement at a Minimum.

❖ Maintain adequate expertise to administer, secure, and monitor network security

❖ Carefully plan network design and architecture in terms of connectivity, placement of key components, and firewalls

❖ Implement a physical security program that controls and limits the access to computing and information resources to only those who absolutely require such access

❖ Incorporate logical access controls to computing and information resources that include a program for issuing user IDs, password requirements, anti-virus programs, and monitoring

❖ Use a login banner to ensure that unauthorized users are warned that they may be subject to monitoring

❖ Report significant unauthorized access attempts to the authorities

❖ Ensure regular use of virus detection software

❖ Monitor employee Internet usage; have policies and guidelines regarding usage.

❖ Turn audit trails on

❖ Trap and Trace - trap and trace means using a device that captures the incoming electronic or other impulses which identify the originating phone number of an instrument or device from which a wire or electronic communication was transmitted from your local telephone company.

❖ Make backups of damaged or altered files

❖ Maintain old backups to show the status of the original

❖ Encrypt files

❖ Encrypt transmissions

❖ Use one-time password generators
❖ Use secure firewalls. Firewall - A system or combination of hardware and software solutions that enforces a boundary between two or more networks
❖ Conduct regular background checks of employees in sensitive positions
❖ Recovery plans should focus on indirect infrastructure threats, as well as the direct attacks against the computer systems and underlying data
❖ Communicate with peers about best practices to protect against identified threats

Process for Cyber Security

A process for Cyber Security includes at a minimum the following steps:

❖ Identify critical assets
❖ Identify and assess vulnerabilities
❖ Normalize, analyze, and prioritize results
❖ Identify which areas offer the greatest risk and decide on alternative solutions
❖ Implement protective programs
❖ Measure performance

Goals and Motivation

The goal of a cyber attack is usually:
❖ Loss of Integrity
❖ Loss of Availability
❖ Loss of Confidentiality
❖ Physical Destruction (i.e. transportation, power, and water companies)

Motivation

Threats to IT systems:
Threat-Source - Motivation Threat Actions
- ❖ **Hackers and Crackers**
    - o Challenge
    - o Ego
    - o Rebellion
    - o Social engineering
    - o System intrusion, break-ins
    - o Unauthorized system access
- ❖ **Computer criminal**
    - o Illegal information disclosure
    - o Monetary gain
    - o Unauthorized data alteration
    - o Computer crime (e.g., cyber stalking)
    - o Fraudulent act (e.g., replay, impersonation, interception)
    - o Information bribery
    - o Spoofing
    - o System intrusion
- ❖ **Attacker**
    - o Blackmail
    - o Destruction
    - o Exploitation
    - o Revenge
    - o Bomb/Terrorism
    - o Information warfare
    - o System attack (e.g., distributed denial of service)
    - o System penetration
    - o System tampering
- ❖ **Industrial espionage** (organizations and governments)
    - o Competitive advantage

- o   Economic espionage
- o   Economic exploitation
- o   Information theft
- o   Intrusion on personal privacy
- o   Social engineering
- o   System penetration
- o   Unauthorized system access (access to classified, proprietary, and/or technology related information)

❖ **Insiders** (poorly trained, disgruntled, malicious, negligent, dishonest, or terminated employees)

- o   Curiosity
- o   Ego
- o   Intelligence
- o   Monetary gain
- o   Revenge
- o   Unintentional errors and omissions (e.g., data entry error, programming error)
- o   Assault on an employee
- o   Blackmail
- o   Browsing of proprietary information
- o   Computer abuse
- o   Fraud and theft
- o   Information bribery
- o   Input of falsified, corrupted data
- o   Interception

❖ **Malicious code** (e.g., virus, logic bomb, Trojan horse)

- o   Sale of personal information
- o   System bugs
- o   System intrusion
- o   System sabotage
- o   Unauthorized system access

Cyber Attack Tools

- ❖ Backdoor: Passing normal security using a hidden method to obtain access to a secured device
  Actions include:
    - Initial turn–up of network elements and/or systems
    - Trouble verification
    - Repair verification
    - Monitor network element (NE) performance
    - Update NE software and hardware
    - Manual control of NE
- ❖ Denial of Service Attacks (DoS): Any attack designed to disrupt service by causing a non-legitimate broadcasting of traffic, resulting in flooding the network
- ❖ Email spoofing the sender, pretending to be someone that they are not, and using social engineering to gain trust
- ❖ IP Address Spoofing: Creating Transmission Control Protocol/Internet Protocol (TCP/IP) packets using another's IP address. This method is often used in DDOS attacks in order to hide the true identity of the attacker
- ❖ Keylogger: Any form of capturing someone's keys, either through logging from software or using a device on hardware
- ❖ Physical Attacks: This involves the actual physical destruction of a computer system and/or network. This includes destroying transport networks, as well as the terminal equipment
- ❖ Sniffer: A program designed to analyze network traffic
- ❖ Trojan Horse: A program or utility that falsely appears to be a useful program or utility, such as a screen saver.

However, once installed, performs a function in the background, such as allowing other users to have access to your computer or sending information from your computer to other computers
❖ Viruses: A software program, script, or macro that has been designed to infect, destroy, modify, or cause other problems with computer or software program

Viruses

There are different types of viruses. Some of these are:

❖ Boot Sector Virus: It is a type of virus that loads up first, just as the computer hard drive gets a chance to complete its initial reloading.
❖ Companion Virus: A companion virus is a malicious file renamed into a legitimate filename in order to load up and infect the machine as a common program gets loaded.
❖ Executable Virus: An executable virus is a kind of malicious software that can run during runtime as a process. This harmful program gets to run its set of instructions to cause harm or compromise to the system.
❖ Overwrite Virus: An overwrite virus overwrites a file, with its own arbitrary instructions, in expectation of continuing to spread throughout the system.
❖ Polymorphic Virus: Usually reprograms itself to evade detection by changing its own coding, generating new signatures that are designed to be stealth to pattern based analysis.
❖ Resident Virus: Remains loaded in the system in order to continue to re-infect the compromised host, to re-infect again if not completely removed.

❖ Stealth Virus: Operates to subvert the system and appear as if everything is running correctly, in order to evade detection.

❖ Worms: Typically spread very rapidly in a network that suffers from the same type of vulnerability. It achieves this by self -replicating itself without any human intervention needed.

❖ Zombie: Compromised computers hijacked and used as a relay point to further attack on behalf of the hacker. These machines are typically a part of a larger group of controlled bot networks for centralized control by the attacker. These hosts usually take part in large-scale denial of service attacks. (DoS)

Chapter 6: Protection

About this Chapter

Knowing what to protect, and knowing options to protect the infrastructure, are key to protecting the information of organizations, clients, and employees.

There are two categories of computer crime. They are criminal activity that involves using a computer to commit a crime, and criminal activity that has a computer as a target. Security Architecture and Design, involves telecommunications, network security, as well as intrusion detection, and is critical in the fight against crime. Physical Security is also important.

Protecting the Data Center

Many years ago, in 2005, CSO Online Magazine had an excellent article by Sarah Scalet on Physical Security for Data Centers. Today, years later, the same sound advice still applies to the structure that houses the technology. Ms. Scalet summarized this difficult task into a short synopsis.

1. Build on the right spot. Be sure the building is some distance from headquarters (20 miles is typical) and at least 100 feet from the main road. Bad neighbors: airports, chemical facilities, power plants. Bad news: earthquake fault lines and areas prone to hurricanes and floods. In addition, scrap the "data center" sign.

2. Have redundant utilities. Data centers need two sources for utilities, such as electricity, water, voice and data. Trace electricity sources back to two separate substations and water back to two different main lines. Lines should be underground and should come into different areas of the building, with water separate from other utilities. Use the data center's anticipated power usage as leverage for getting the electric company to accommodate the building's special needs.

3. Pay attention to walls. Foot-thick concrete is a cheap and effective barrier against the elements and explosive devices. For extra security, use walls lined with Kevlar.

4. Avoid windows. Think of how a warehouse is without windows. If you must have windows, limit them to the break room or administrative area, and use bomb-resistant laminated glass.

5. Use landscaping for protection. Trees, boulders and gulleys can hide the building from passing cars, obscure security devices (like fences), and also help keep vehicles from getting too close. Oh, and they look nice too.

6. Keep a 100-foot buffer zone around the site. Where landscaping does not protect the building from vehicles, use crash-proof barriers instead. Bollard planters are less conspicuous and more attractive than other devices.

7. Use retractable crash barriers at vehicle entry points. Control access to the parking lot and loading dock with a staffed guard station that operates the retractable bollards. Use a raised gate and a green light as visual cues that the bollards are down and the driver can go forward. In situations when extra security is needed, have the barriers left up by default, and lowered only when someone has permission to pass through."

One of the most important measures taken during forensics gathering is in the protection of evidence. In order for the evidence to be admissible in court, a chain-of-custody has to be proven to be properly managed and maintained. This document is establishing accountability by logging each person who gets to obtain the evidence. This is important in order to prevent evidence tampering and to prove that the integrity of the evidence has not been broken and that the collections at hand were properly preserved.

Intrusion Detection

Intrusion Detection is the art of detecting inappropriate, incorrect, or anomalous activity. Among other tools, an Intrusion Detection System (IDS) can be used to determine if a computer network or server has experienced an unauthorized intrusion.

An Intrusion Detection System provides much the same purpose as a burglar alarm system installed in a house. In case of a (possible) intrusion, the IDS system will issue some type of warning or alert. An operator will then tag events of interest for further investigation by the Incident Handling team.

An Intrusion Detection system (IDS) generally detects unwanted manipulations of computer systems, mainly through the Internet. The manipulations may take the form of attacks by crackers.

An Intrusion Detection system is used to detect several types of malicious behaviors that can compromise the security and trust of a computer system. This includes network attacks against vulnerable services, data driven attacks on applications, host based attacks such as privilege escalation, unauthorized logins and access to sensitive files, and malware (viruses, trojan horses, and worms).

An IDS is composed of several components: Sensors, which generate security events, a Console to monitor events and alerts and control the sensors, and a central Engine that records events logged by the sensors in a database and uses a system of rules to generate alerts from security events received. There are several ways to categorize an IDS depending on the type and location of the sensors and the methodology used by the engine to generate alerts. In many simple IDS implementations all three components are combined in a single device or appliance."

IDS's are used for monitoring packets in order to view the packets as they occur, in contrast to IPS's which typically operate within in-line mode where the appliance has the capability to drop malicious traffic in real-time.

Four Types of IDS/IPS

Four types of IDS/IPS technologies:

- ❖ Network based Intrusion Detection System (NIDS) monitors the network
- ❖ Wireless monitors wireless network traffic and analyzes it to identify suspicious activity involving the wireless networking protocols themselves
- ❖ Network Behavior Analysis (NBA) identifies threats that generate unusual traffic flows by examining network traffic

❖ Host based Intrusion Detection System (HIDS) monitors single host characteristics and monitors within the host for suspicious activity

Honeypots

A honeypot is designed to lure attackers away from the real network. This is done to better understand the attack vector by a machine left purposely exposed in order to be observed. Honeypots are designed not to possess any real valuable or legitimate data or resources. It is used as a tool in order to help track down cyber criminals for prosecution.

There are two general types of honeypots:

❖ Production honeypots are easy to use, capture only limited information, and are used primarily by companies or corporations
❖ Research honeypots are complex to deploy and maintain, capture extensive information, and are used primarily by research, military, or government organizations
Source: Honeypots.net

Some key concerns are:
❖ Secure cyberspace
❖ Detecting and interpreting attacks against large-scale network infrastructures
❖ Evaluating the use of tools in many different environments
❖ Performing static and dynamic analysis of software to discover vulnerabilities
❖ Analyzing and modeling computer networks attacks and potential propagation vectors

- ❖ Correlating and prioritizing alerts from network security devices
- ❖ Designing and developing practical cryptographic protocols and approaches

Cyber security solutions must be all-encompassing and cover the following areas at a minimum:

- ❖ Access Control
- ❖ Application Security
- ❖ Cryptography
- ❖ Information Security and Risk Management
- ❖ Legal, Regulations, Compliance and Investigations
- ❖ Operations Security
- ❖ Physical (Environmental) Security
- ❖ Security Architecture and Design
- ❖ Telecommunications and Network Security

Note: Business Continuity and Disaster Recovery Planning must take place to assist the Business functions to respond to impacts caused by a Cyber event.

Security Information and Event Management

Fundamentally, Security Information and Event Management (SIEM) is a strategic approach to security management that aims to paint a holistic picture of an organization's information technology (IT) security. It combines Security Information Management (SIM) and Security Event Management (SEM).

SIEM services deliver real-time analysis of security alerts generated from network hardware and applications. The services may include logging security data and generating reports to meet compliance standards.

A key focus is monitoring and helping to manage user and service privileges, directory services, and various other system configuration changes; as well as delivering log auditing and reviewing events.

- ❖ Alerting: is executed via automated analysis of correlated events and production of alerts, in order to notify recipients of urgent issues. Alerting can be done directly to a dashboard, or transmitted via third party channels, such as email.
- ❖ Compliance: Applications can be harnessed to automate the collection of compliance data, generating reports that adapt to existing security, governance, and auditing processes.
- ❖ Correlation: seeks common attributes, and links events together into meaningful bundles. This technology is able to perform a variety of correlation techniques, integrating various sources to turn data into useful usable information. Correlation is normally a function of the Security Event Management part of a full SIEM solution.
- ❖ Dashboards: Tools take event data and convert it into informational charts to assist in recognizing patterns, or identify an activity that is not considered a typical standard pattern.
- ❖ Data aggregation: Log management aggregates data from various sources, such as network, security, servers, databases and applications, resulting in the

capability to consolidate monitored data to help avoid missing crucial events.

❖ Forensic analysis: The important functionality of searching across logs on different nodes and time periods based on specified criteria. This mitigates aggregation of log information in one's head or the need to search through thousands upon thousands of logs and data.

❖ Retention: This is important for long-term storage of historical data to facilitate correlation of data over time, providing the necessary tools for compliance. Long-term log data retention is important for forensic investigations, as it's highly unlikely that discovery of network breaches happen in real-time.

The underlying principle of a SIEM system is that crucial data concerning an enterprise's security architecture is generated in multiple locations, with the ability to observe all the data from a single point of view, making it easier to both identify trends and recognize patterns that appear out of the ordinary. SIEM is the powerful combination of SIM (Security Information Management) and SEM (Security Event Management) functions into one security management system.

A SEM system is able to centralize the storage and interpretation of logs, allowing for near real-time analysis, enabling security personnel to execute the right countermeasure quickly and decisively. A SIM system has the ability to collect data into a central repository for trend analysis, generating automated reporting for compliance and centralized reporting.

By marrying these two vital functions together, SIEM systems are able to produce quicker identification, analysis, and recovery of security events. They also serve an important role for compliance managers to confirm they are meeting and fulfilling an organization's legal compliance requirements.

Summary:

Managing information, computers, and physical systems is becoming more important in the exponential need of security. As technology advances, so does the need for improved security practices, in order to protect these systems. Societies depend heavily on all types of computing power to function in their daily lives. Security deals with the threats and dangers that leave systems vulnerable to compromise and exploitation.

Chapter 7: Self-Assessment Tests

Chapter 1 Test

1. Which ISO/IEC series covers an overview and vocabulary relating to Information Technology, Security Technique and Information Security Management Systems?

2. Which Standard relates to Health Insurance information?

3. Which critical infrastructure protection plan addresses the security of cyber assets essential to the reliable operation of the electric grid?

4. Which requirements are a set of comprehensive requirements for enhancing payment account data security?

5. What is COBIT?

6. What does the European Union Agency for Network and Information Security (ENISA) maintain?

Chapter 2 Test

1. What are key questions to ask yourself before starting to plan?

2. If there is a Cyber Security Plan in place, what are key questions to ask?

Chapter 3 Test

1. Why have a Cyber Security program?

2. Why are Cyber attacks becoming a viable option instead of traditional physical acts of violence?

3. What is one of the best ways to protect information or physical property?

4. What is one thing that is important for antivirus software to be effective?

Chapter 4 Test

1. What was the first United Nations-backed cybersecurity alliance?

2. When did the United States and China sign a Cyber Agreement?

3. When did the Council of Europe (CoE) Cybercrime go into force?

4. What is the name of the Programs, Plans, and Procedures that enable an organization to respond to a Cyber Incident that can threaten the organization, information, and clients?

Chapter 5 Test

1. What are forms of Cyber-attacker attacks?

2. What is a Critical Infrastructure?

3. What are some reasons for Cyber Attacks by a Computer Criminal?

Chapter 6 Test

1. What are two categories of Computer Crime?

2. What are four types of IDS/IPS technologies?

3. What is a honeypot?

4. What is the underlying principle of SIEM?

Chapter 8: Self-Assessment Tests (Answers)

Chapter 1 Test

1. **Which ISO/IEC series covers an overview and vocabulary relating to Information Technology, Security Technique and Information Security Management Systems?**

   ISO 27000:20XX

2. **Which Standard relates to Health Insurance Information?**

   Health Insurance Portability and Accountability Act (HIPAA)

3. **Which critical infrastructure protection plan addresses the security of cyber assets essential to the reliable operation of the electric grid?**

   North American Electric Reliability Corporation Critical Infrastructure Plan (NERC CIP)

4. **Which requirements are a set of comprehensive requirements for enhancing payment account data security?**

   Payment Card Industry Data Security Standard (PCI DSS)

5. **What is COBIT**

   COBIT 4.1 is an IT governance framework and supporting toolset that allows managers to bridge the gap between control requirements, technical issues and business risks

COBIT 5 consolidates and integrates the COBIT 4.1, Val IT 2.0 and Risk IT frameworks and also draws significantly from the Business Model for Information Security (BMIS) and ITAF

6. **What does the European Union Agency for Network and Information Security (ENISA) maintain?**

Maintains a list of National Cyber Security Strategy Documents in the EU. and in addition, includes many other non-EU countries.

Chapter 2 Test

1. **What are key questions to ask yourself before starting to plan?**

Who are the key members?

Who should be included?

What information does the organization not want employees accessing from home?

What are some "how to" areas that have to be considered from a documentation point of view?

2. **If there is a Cyber Security Plan in place, what are key questions to ask?**

Does information considered critical by the organization include security mitigation, protection, and recoverability of data?

Does it identify teams needed?

Has the plan ever been tested along with the Continuity Plan?

How are team members selected?

How are vendors Cyber Security Plans evaluated?

How many times has the organization tested the security in a secure environment as opposed to a mock disaster where chaos is an added factor in the security testing?

Is mandatory continued education included?

Chapter 3 Test

1. Why have a Cyber Security program?

Cyber security involves protecting that information by detecting, preventing and responding to attacks. It is a development of processes and best practices designed to protect networks, computers, programs and data damage or unauthorized access.

2. Why are Cyber attacks becoming a viable option instead of traditional physical acts of violence?

Anonymity
Diverse targets
Low risk of detection
Low risk of personal injury

Low investment
Operate from nearly any location
Few resources are needed

3. **What is one of the best ways to protect information or physical property?**

Ensure that only authorized people have access to it.

4. **What is one thing that is important for antivirus software to be effective?**

It must be kept current with daily signature-database updates. It is also important to use the most recent engine, because new methods of detection and removal are found only in the most current versions of antivirus software.

Chapter 4 Test

1. **What was the first United Nations-backed cybersecurity alliance?**

The International Multilateral Partnership Against Cyber Threats (IMPACT) is the first United Nations-backed cybersecurity alliance. This was the first international treaty on crimes committed via the Internet.

2. **When did the United States and China sign a Cyber Agreement?**

September 25, 2015.

3. **When did the Council of Europe (CoE) Cybercrime go into force?**

July 1, 2004.

4. What is the name of the Programs, Plans, and Procedures that enable an organization to respond to a Cyber Incident that can threaten the organization, information, and clients?

Cyber Security Incident Response (CSIRT)

Chapter 5 Test

1. What are forms of Cyber-attacker attacks?

Denial or disruption of computer, cable, satellite, or telecommunications services

Disclosure of private, classified or proprietary information communicated or stored within computer, cable, satellite or telecommunications systems

Modification or destruction of computer programming codes, computer network databases, stored information, or computer capabilities

Manipulation of computer, cable, satellite, or telecommunications services resulting in fraud, financial loss or other criminal violation

Threats to destroy data or program files

2. What is a Critical Infrastructure?

Critical Infrastructures are those systems or assets, whether physical or virtual, that if debilitated or incapacitated would have a debilitating effect. This is an area most threatened and easily fits within the targeted criteria of an attacker.

3. What are some reasons for Cyber Attacks by a Computer Criminal?

Illegal information disclosure
Monetary gain
Unauthorized data alteration
Computer crime (e.g., cyber stalking)
Fraudulent act (e.g., replay, impersonation, interception)
Information bribery
Spoofing
System intrusion

Chapter 6 Test

1. What are two categories of Computer Crime?

Criminal activity that involves using a computer to commit a crime
Criminal activity that has a computer as a target

2. What are four types of IDS/IPS technologies?

Network based Intrusion Detection System (NIDS) monitors the network.

Wireless monitors wireless network traffic and analyzes it to identify suspicious activity involving the wireless networking protocols themselves

Network Behavior Analysis (NBA) identifies threats that generate unusual traffic flows by examining network traffic

Host based Intrusion Detection System (HIDS) monitors single host characteristics and monitors within the host for suspicious activity

3. What is a honeypot?

A honeypot is designed to lure attackers away from the real network in order to better understand the attack vector by a machine purposely left exposed in order to be observed. Honeypots are designed not to possess any real valuable or legitimate data or resources. It is used as a tool in order to help track down cyber criminals for prosecution.

4. What is the underlying principle of SIEM?

Crucial data concerning an enterprise's security architecture is generated in multiple locations and with the ability to observe all the data from a single point of view makes it easier to identify trends and to recognize patterns that appear out of the ordinary.

Dear Reader,

Thank you so much for going on this journey through Mastering Your Introduction to Cyber Security with me. I wish you continued success in the field.

Please continue to read the next sections for a special offer just for my readers.

Michael

Contact the Author

Dr. Michael C. Redmond, PhD
msmichaelredmond@redmondworldwide.com

Connect with me on LinkedIn

LinkedIn Profile

https://www.linkedin.com/in/michaelredmond2018

Website

www.redmondworldwide.com

Twitter

@msmredmond

Cell 917-882-5453

Michael C. Redmond

Cyber Security Audio Training

Is provided on a USB Flash Drive

Order my Audio Training at a discounted rate because you have completed reading *Mastering Your Introduction to Cyber Security* and are now ready for the next step in mastering your introduction.

- 6 Sections Plus a printable Workbook
- 6 Continuing Ed Points from DRII for those certified in Business Continuity; for other certifications contact the certifying body.

See more information at www.redmondworldwide.com under "Educational Audio Training" tab. Or go to **www.rwknowledge.com**
Order your Cyber Audio training on my site today at a discounted rate.
Use Code: Cyberbook

Or simply call "Fred" and tell him you want your discount for reading *Mastering Your Introduction to Cyber Security*. 1-213-718-7303

On my site it sells for $195. **Your special rate is $145. Use Code Cyberbook**

Michael C. Redmond

Cyber Security Audio Training

Is provided on a USB Flash Drive

Contents

Policy

Application Security

Common Exploits

Security testing for applications

Session Three

Incident Reporting and Response Planning and Recovery Plans

Information Security and Risk Management

Basic Principles of Information Security

- Confidentiality, Integrity, Availability
- Risk Management
- Types of Controls
- Security Classification for Information
- Access Control
- Cryptography

Information security as a process

- Security Planning
- Incident Response Plans
- Change Management
- Disaster Recovery Planning

Steps in the risk management process
- Establish the Context
- Identification
- Assessment
- Risk Mitigation Plan
- Implementation
- Review and Evaluation of the Plan

Areas of risk management
- Enterprise risk management
- Project Management

Session Four

Operations Security

Counter Intelligence

Information Security (InfoSec)

Transmission Security (TRANSEC)

Communications Security (COMSEC)

Signal Security (SIGSEC)

Systems Security

Physical (Environmental) Security

Elements

Look for my other books in my Mastering Series

- Mastering Business Continuity Planning
- Mastering Work Life Balance

Sign up for my newsletter at www.redmondworldwide.com